I0876378

AMERICAN CITIES

SEATTLE

Jacqueline S. Cotton

LET'S READ AV² BY WEIGL™ ADDED VALUE • AUDIO VISUAL

www.av2books.com

Go to **www.av2books.com**, and enter this book's unique code.

BOOK CODE

AVB92878

AV² by Weigl brings you media enhanced books that support active learning.

AV² provides enriched content that supplements and complements this book. Weigl's AV² books strive to create inspired learning and engage young minds in a total learning experience.

Your AV² Media Enhanced books come alive with...

Audio
Listen to sections of the book read aloud.

Video
Watch informative video clips.

Embedded Weblinks
Gain additional information for research.

Try This!
Complete activities and hands-on experiments.

Key Words
Study vocabulary, and complete a matching word activity.

Quizzes
Test your knowledge.

Slide Show
View images and captions, and prepare a presentation.

... and much, much more!

Published by AV² by Weigl
350 5th Avenue, 59th Floor New York, NY 10118
Website: www.av2books.com

Library of Congress Cataloging-in-Publication Data

Names: Cotton, Jacqueline S., author.
Title: Seattle / Jacqueline S. Cotton.
Description: New York, NY : AV2 by Weigl, [2018] | Series: American cities | Audience: Grades K-3.
Identifiers: LCCN 2018048670 (print) | LCCN 2018049049 (ebook) | ISBN 9781489694744 (Multi User ebook) | ISBN 9781489694782 (Single User ebook) | ISBN 9781489694720 (hardcover : alk. paper) | ISBN 9781489694737 (softcover)
Subjects: LCSH: Seattle (Wash.)--Juvenile literature.
Classification: LCC F899.S44 (ebook) | LCC F899.S44 C68 2018 (print) | DDC 979.7/772--dc23
LC record available at https://lccn.loc.gov/2018048670

Printed in the United States of America in Brainerd, Minnesota
1 2 3 4 5 6 7 8 9 0 22 21 20 19 18

112018
051118

Project Coordinator: Heather Kissock Designer: Ana María Vidal

Weigl acknowledges Getty Images, Alamy, Shutterstock, and iStock as the primary image suppliers for this title. Museum of History and Industry: page 20R.

Contents

Get to Know Seattle

Seattle is the largest city in the state of Washington. It is sometimes called the "Emerald City." This is because of all the plants that grow there. Seattle's many forests and parks make the city look green year-round.

Map of Washington

Where Is Seattle?

Seattle is in the northwest part of the state. It is 61 miles northeast of Washington's capital city, Olympia. You can get to Olympia from Seattle by traveling southwest on the I-5 highway.

There are many other exciting places to visit in Washington. You can use a road map to plan a trip. Which roads could you take from Seattle to get to these places? How long might it take you to get to each one?

TRAVELING WASHINGTON
Seattle to Snoqualmie 29 miles
Seattle to Olympic National Park 74 miles
Seattle to San Juan Islands 109 miles
Seattle to Lake Chelan 198 miles

Climate

Seattle is a rainy city. It gets about 37 inches of rain a year. Most of this rain falls during the winter months.

Summers in Seattle are drier and warm. Days are often cloudy. The city has fewer than 60 days of sunshine every year.

Seattle has about **150 rainy days** every year.

Population and Geography

More than 700,000 people live in Seattle. Another 3 million people live in the area around the city. Seattle is one of the fastest growing cities in the country.

Seattle is surrounded by several mountains. Mount Rainier lies to the south of the city. At 14,410 feet tall, it is the highest mountain in the state. Mount Rainier is also an active volcano.

Many Peoples

Native Americans were the first people to live in what is now Seattle. In 1851, a group of settlers arrived from Illinois. They soon built a small town on the land.

In 1896, gold was found in northern Canada. People from all over the world came to Seattle to begin the trip north. Many of these people came back to Seattle to live. The city has continued to grow ever since.

In **1890**, Seattle had a **population** of about **49,000**. By **1910**, more than **230,000** people lived there.

SCHWABA
1
S.S.
TENNIAL.

PUBLIC
MARKET
CENTER
MEET
FARMERS MA
YOUR CHANGE
CHANGES LIVES!
DONATE HERE!
Copper River
Salmon

Tourism

Millions of tourists flock to Seattle's Pike Place Market every year. Open since 1907, this is the oldest farmers' market in the city. It offers shops, restaurants, and fresh produce.

The Space Needle is Seattle's best-known landmark. People can take an elevator ride to the top of the tower. Here, they can view the city and its nearby mountains and lakes.

The ride to the **top** of the **Space Needle** takes only **43 seconds**.

Sports

Seattle is home to five major sports teams. The Mariners play baseball at Safeco Field. Football fans enjoy watching the Seahawks play at CenturyLink Field.

People go to Sounders games to watch men's soccer. The women's soccer team is called the Reign. The Storm play women's basketball for the city.

SEAHAWKS
3
SEAHAWKS
65
65
65
SEAHAWKS

SSA TERMINALS
SSA TERMINALS
SSA TERMINALS
SSATerminals
Tropical
Tropical
Tropical
MAERSK
MAERSK
MAERSK
MAERSK
MAERSK
MAERSK
SEALAND
CMA CGM
CMA CGM
CMA CGM
ADRIAN MÆRSK
DRAGØR

Economy

Seattle is home to many companies that are known worldwide. Microsoft is a technology company. Amazon sells products over the internet.

Seattle is an important port city as well. Ferries take people to nearby islands. Cruise ships take tourists to Alaska. Cargo ships pick up goods in Seattle and take them to other parts of the world.

Every time a **cruise ship docks in Seattle**, it brings about **$2.7 million** to the city.

Seattle Timeline

12,000 years ago
Native Americans live on the land now known as Seattle.

1851
Settlers from Illinois arrive in the area.

1869
Seattle becomes a city.

1889
The Great Seattle Fire destroys the city's downtown.

1911
The Port of Seattle is founded.

1961
The Space Needle is built for the 1962 World's Fair.

2014
The Seattle Seahawks win the Super Bowl.

2017
Pike Place Market opens its new $74 million MarketFront expansion.

Things to Do in Seattle

Seattle Center Monorail
Go for a ride on this train that links the Space Needle to the city's downtown. It can reach a speed of 45 miles per hour as it weaves its way above the city streets.

Pacific Science Center
Visitors to this science center can launch rockets at the Tinker Tank and walk past exhibits about dinosaurs that lived long ago.

Seattle Aquarium

The Seattle Aquarium's animals are housed in several large exhibits. One exhibit has a 120,000-gallon tank filled with sea life from the area.

International District

Asian culture is on full display in Seattle's International District. The many Asian shops and restaurants are popular places to visit.

Seattle Great Wheel

Built in 2012, this 175-foot-tall Ferris wheel gives people great views of the city.

KEY WORDS

Research has shown that as much as 65 percent of all written material published in English is made up of 300 words. These 300 words cannot be taught using pictures or learned by sounding them out. They must be recognized by sight. This book contains 110 common sight words to help young readers improve their reading fluency and comprehension. This book also teaches young readers several important content words, such as proper nouns. These words are paired with pictures to aid in learning and improve understanding.

Page	Sight Words First Appearance
4	get, know, to
5	all, and, because, city, grow, in, is, it, look, make, many, of, plants, sometimes, state, that, the, there, this, year
7	a, are, by, can, could, each, from, how, long, might, miles, on, one, other, part, places, take, these, use, where, which, you
8	about, days, every, has, most, often, than
11	also, an, another, around, at, country, feet, live, more, mountains, people
12	back, begin, came, first, found, group, had, land, now, over, small, soon, they, was, were, what, world
15	here, its, only, open
16	for, go, home, men, play, watch
19	as, goods, important, them, time, up, well
20	great
21	new
22	above, do, things, walk, way
23	animals, gives, housed, large, life, with

Page	Content Words First Appearance
4	Seattle
5	forests, parks, Washington
7	highway, Olympia, road map, trip
8	climate, inches, months, rain, summers, sunshine
11	area, geography, Mount Rainier, population, volcano
12	Canada, gold, Illinois, Native Americans, settlers, town
15	farmers' market, lakes, landmark, Pike Place Market, produce, restaurants, ride, seconds, shops, Space Needle, top, tourism, tourists, tower
16	baseball, basketball, CenturyLink Field, fans, games, Mariners, Reign, Safeco Field, Seahawks, soccer, sports, Storm, teams
19	Alaska, Amazon, companies, economy, ferries, internet, islands, Microsoft, products, ships
20	downtown, Great Seattle Fire, timeline
21	expansion, Super Bowl, World's Fair
22	dinosaurs, exhibits, hour, Pacific Science Center, rockets, Seattle Center Monorail, speed, streets, Tinker Tank, train, visitors
23	culture, display, Ferris wheel, International District, Seattle Aquarium, Seattle Great Wheel, tank, views

Check out www.av2books.com for activities, videos, audio clips, and more!

1. **Go to www.av2books.com.**
2. **Enter book code.** AVB92878
3. **Fuel your imagination online!**

www.av2books.com